CAN I BE SURE
I'm SAVED?

The Crucial Questions Series By R.C. Sproul

Free digital editions available at ReformationTrust.com/FreeCQ

Crucial
Questions
No. 7

CAN I BE SURE
I'm SAVED?

R.C. SPROUL

IR *Reformation Trust*   A DIVISION OF LIGONIER MINISTRIES, ORLANDO, FL

Can I Be Sure I'm Saved?

© 2010 by R.C. Sproul

Published by Reformation Trust Publishing
a division of Ligonier Ministries
421 Ligonier Court, Sanford, FL 32771
Ligonier.org   ReformationTrust.com

Printed in North Mankato, MN
Corporate Graphics
May 2016

First edition, fifteenth printing

Cover design: Gearbox Studios
Interior design and typeset: Katherine Lloyd, The DESK

Unless otherwise noted, Scripture quotations are from *The Holy Bible, English Standard Version*®, copyright © 2001 by Crossway Bibles, a publishing ministry of Good News Publishers. Used by permission. All rights reserved.

Scripture quotations marked NKJV are from the *New King James Version*®, Copyright © 1982 by Thomas Nelson. Used by permission. All rights reserved.

Scripture quotations marked NASB are from the *New American Standard Bible*®, copyright © 1960, 1962, 1963, 1968, 1971, 1972, 1973, 1975, 1995 by The Lockman Foundation. Used by permission. (www.Lockman.org)

Library of Congress Cataloging-in-Publication Data
Sproul, R. C. (Robert Charles), 1939-
  Can I be sure I'm saved? / R. C. Sproul.
     p. cm.
  ISBN 978-1-56769-208-2
  1. Assurance (Theology) I. Title.
  BT785.S67 2010
  234--dc22

                                    2010008924

Contents

Chapter One

THE STRUGGLE
FOR ASSURANCE

There is a passage in the New Testament that I believe is one of the most terrifying in the Bible. It comes from the lips of Jesus at the end of the Sermon on the Mount.

We tend to think of the Sermon on the Mount as a positive proclamation by our Lord. After all, it is in the Sermon on the Mount that He gives the Beatitudes: "Blessed are the poor in spirit. . . . Blessed are those who mourn. . . . Blessed are the meek . . . ," and so on (Matt. 5:3–12). Because of the Sermon on the Mount, Jesus has a reputation as a preacher who accents the positive rather than the negative.

But we often overlook the climax of that sermon, where Jesus says:

"Not everyone who says to me, 'Lord, Lord,' will enter the kingdom of heaven, but the one who does the will of my Father who is in heaven. On that day many will say to me, 'Lord, Lord, did we not prophesy in your name, and cast out demons in your name, and do many mighty works in your name?' And then will I declare to them, 'I never knew you; depart from me, you workers of lawlessness.'" (Matt. 7:21–23)

Here Jesus gives us a preview of the last judgment. He says that people will come to Him, addressing Him by the title "Lord." They will say to Jesus: "Lord, we did many marvelous things in Your name. We served You; we preached in Your name; we cast out demons; we did all of these things." Jesus says, "I will turn to these people and say, 'Please leave.'" Not only will He say, "I don't know you," but, "I never knew you, you workers of lawlessness."

What is particularly poignant about this terrifying — deeply moving warning is that He begins by saying, "Not everyone who says to me, 'Lord, Lord,' will enter the kingdom of heaven." Then He repeats that by saying, "On that day many will say to me, 'Lord, Lord.'"

"Lord, Lord"

There are only about fifteen occurrences in all of Scripture where someone is addressed by the repetition of his or her name. Let me mention a few:

• Abraham on Mount Moriah was ready to plunge the knife into the chest of his son Isaac, and God intervened at the last second, saying to him through the angel of the Lord: "Abraham, Abraham! . . . Do not lay your hand on the boy" (Gen. 22:11–12).

• Jacob was afraid to go down into Egypt, and God came to reassure him, saying, "Jacob, Jacob" (Gen. 46:2).

• God spoke to Moses out of the burning bush at Mount Horeb, saying, "Moses, Moses!" (Ex. 3:4).

• God called to the boy Samuel in the middle of the night, saying, "Samuel! Samuel!" (1 Sam. 3:10).

• Jesus, when rebuking Martha in Bethany, said to her, "Martha, Martha" (Luke 10:41).

• Jesus lamented over the city of Jerusalem and cried out: "O Jerusalem, Jerusalem, the city that kills the prophets and stones those who are sent to it! How often would I have gathered your children together as a hen gathers her brood under her wings, and you would not!" (Luke 13:34).

• Peter said he would be strong in all circumstances, and Jesus said, "Simon, Simon, behold, Satan demanded to have you, that he might sift you like wheat" (Luke 22:31).

• Jesus confronted Saul on the road to Damascus, saying, "Saul, Saul, why are you persecuting me?" (Acts 9:4).

• Perhaps the most poignant example of this repetition in Scripture is found in Jesus' cry from the cross: "My God, my God, why have you forsaken me?" (Matt. 27:46).

This rare grammatical structure has significance in the Hebrew language. When someone repeats the personal form of address, it suggests and communicates an intimate personal relationship with the person to whom he is speaking.

So Jesus says here in the Sermon on the Mount that on the last day, not only will people come to Him and say, "Lord, we belong to you, we're yours," but they will address Him in terms of personal intimacy. They will say, "Lord, Lord," as if they know Him in a deep, personal way. But despite this assumption of an intimate relationship, Jesus will say to them: "Please leave. I don't know you workers of lawlessness."

Jesus is saying that there are many people who profess to be Christians, who use the name of Christ, and who call Him by His exalted title "Lord" but actually are not in the kingdom of God at all. They do not belong to Him and will not be able to stand at the last judgment. The terrifying aspect of this is that these people are not on the fringes of the church. Rather, they are immersed in the life of the church, heavily involved in ministry, and perhaps have the reputation of being professing Christians. Yet Jesus doesn't know them and will banish them from His presence.

I bring this up at the beginning of this booklet because when we make a profession of faith as Christians, we have to ask ourselves a question: How do we *know* that we won't be among this group of people who will come at the last judgment, expecting entrance into the kingdom and addressing Jesus in intimate terms, only to be cast out? How do we know that our confidence that we are in a state of grace is not misplaced? How do we know we have not deceived ourselves? How can we be sure we are saved?

A Controversial Doctrine

For centuries, the question of assurance has sparked controversy in the church. Many churches have gone so far as to question whether assurance is even attainable.

For example, at the Council of Trent in the sixteenth century, the Roman Catholic Church denied that it is possible for a person to have assurance of salvation except in rare circumstances. Rome went on to teach that the only people who can rise to assurance of their salvation in this life are exceptional saints to whom God gives a special revelation of their status before Him. However, the average member of the church cannot expect to have assurance of salvation.

Rome claims that most "assurances," in the final analysis, are based on conjecture, opinion, and ideas that come from the hearts of people whom the Bible defines as deeply rooted in deceit. The Scriptures tell us that the heart is deceitful above all things (Jer. 17:9), so it is easy for us, Rome says, to deceive ourselves and to rest our confidence about the state of our souls on mere opinion. Consequently, assurance of salvation is not possible apart from some special act of revelation.

It is not only the Roman Catholic Church that denies

the doctrine of the assurance of salvation. Some Protestants believe that a person can have assurance of salvation for today but no assurance for tomorrow, because they accept the possibility that people who have faith at one time can fall away into faithlessness and lose their salvation. That's why, historically, the doctrine of the assurance of salvation has been tied closely to the doctrine of the perseverance of the saints. So whereas Rome says we cannot have assurance at all, these Protestants say we can have assurance for a limited time, but we cannot know what our ultimate state is going to be.

Then there is Reformed theology, my own theological persuasion, which teaches that we not only can know today that we are in a state of grace, but that we can have full assurance that we still will be in a state of grace at the times of our deaths.

The Parable of the Sower

Jesus addresses the question of who is and is not genuinely saved in His parable of the sower:

> That same day Jesus went out of the house and sat beside the sea. And great crowds gathered about

him, so that he got into a boat and sat down. And the whole crowd stood on the beach. And he told them many things in parables, saying: "A sower went out to sow. And as he sowed, some seeds fell along the path, and the birds came and devoured them. Other seeds fell on rocky ground, where they did not have much soil, and immediately they sprang up, since they had no depth of soil, but when the sun rose they were scorched. And since they had no root, they withered away. Other seeds fell among thorns, and the thorns grew up and choked them. Other seeds fell on good soil and produced grain, some a hundredfold, some sixty, some thirty. He who has ears, let him hear." (Matt. 13:1–9)

It is important to note the context of this famous parable. Just before it, someone says to Jesus, "Behold, Your mother and Your brothers are standing outside seeking to speak to You" (Matt. 12:47, NASB). But Jesus answers, "Who is My mother and who are My brothers?" (v. 48, NASB). Then, indicating His disciples, He says: "Behold My mother and My brothers! For whoever does the will of My Father who is in heaven, he is My brother and sister and mother" (vv. 49–50, NASB). Jesus says that His true brother is the one who does the will of the Father, not one who simply makes a decision to follow Him.

We should always keep in mind that nobody forced Judas to become a disciple. Judas chose to follow Jesus; he made his own decision to enter the school of Jesus, and he stayed with our Lord during His earthly ministry for three years. Yet we are told that he was a devil (John 6:70). It wasn't that Judas was genuinely converted and then fell out of grace and was lost; rather, although he was close to Jesus, he was never a converted man. That ought to give us pause as we consider the states of our own souls.

A little later in the book of Matthew, Jesus gives an explanation of His parable of the sower. It is one of the rare times in the Gospel accounts where we are given an explanation of a parable. That explanation is most helpful because this parable differs from normal parabolic instruction. Most parables have just one point. It is generally dangerous, therefore, to turn parables into allegories, which tend to have symbolic meanings sprinkled throughout the story. But the parable of the sower approaches the level of an allegory as Jesus makes several points of application.

Jesus begins His explanation by saying: "Hear then the

parable of the sower: When anyone hears the word of the kingdom and does not understand it, the evil one comes and snatches away what has been sown in his heart. This is what was sown along the path" (Matt. 13:18–19). The first group He is talking about is represented by the seed that fell on the path. In antiquity, at planting time, a farmer sowed his seed first, then plowed the ground. But any seed that fell on a roadway or pathway was not plowed under. Lying on the hardened path, it had no way to take root, and was devoured by birds. Jesus likens the birds to Satan. Many people are like this seed. They hear the preaching of the gospel, but it makes no impact on them. It does not take root in their lives.

Jesus continues, "As for what was sown on rocky ground, this is the one who hears the word and immediately receives it with joy, yet he has no root in himself, but endures for a while, and when tribulation or persecution arises on account of the word, immediately he falls away" (vv. 20–21).

If you go to an evangelistic meeting or watch one on TV, you may see huge crowds thronging to the front of the church in response to the call of the gospel. In fact, I once saw a report about a massive international evangelistic campaign in which millions of people supposedly had made decisions for Christ. When I read that, I wondered how many of those decisions for Christ were true conversions and how many of them were spurious. People like what they hear at these events and can be emotionally moved to make a decision to follow Christ. However, it is an established fact that many of those who come forward at evangelistic meetings soon abandon their commitments altogether. Their spur-of-the-moment responses are often groundless.

I don't want to be too harsh in my response to reports about the successes of evangelistic events. I recognize that all outreach ministries face the problem of measuring their effectiveness. Churches generally do it by reporting the number of members in their congregations and how much they have grown over a period of time. Evangelistic ministries often do it by reporting the number of people who come to the front, raise a hand, sign a card, or pray a prayer. These ministries want to have some kind of statistic to measure the response people are making.

But how does one measure a spiritual reality? Anyone who has been involved in evangelism knows that we cannot see the heart, so the next best thing is to count the number of decisions that people make. But Jesus warns us about that here in the parable of the sower when He says that *many* people hear the gospel with joy—but they don't continue in the faith. This second type of seed falls on stony ground—ground that is so shallow the seed cannot put down roots, and as soon as the sun comes up, the seedlings begin to wither. The result is that they die away and never bear fruit. Jesus tells us that these people fall away because of the tribulations and persecutions that inevitably arise in the way of faith.

Explaining the third type of seed, Jesus says, "As for what was sown among thorns, this is the one who hears the word, but the cares of the world and the deceitfulness of riches choke the word, and it proves unfruitful" (Matt. 13:22). This seed represents a category of people who also hear and receive the Word, but who are overwhelmed by the cares of this world. Like thorns, worldly cares "choke the word."

Lastly, Jesus says: "As for what was sown on good soil, this is the one who hears the word and understands it. He indeed bears fruit" (Matt. 13:23a).

Clearly, then, there are many who respond to the message of the gospel with joy but ultimately do not continue in the faith. Not everyone who hears the Word of God is saved, and the same is true for many who respond to it initially. Those who are genuinely saved are those who prove themselves to be doers of the Word. When the seed takes root and grows, there is fruit.

The Need for Fruit

In thinking about fruitfulness, we must remember that we are not saved by our works. Rather, we are justified by faith alone. Yet we also remember that the magisterial Reformers of the sixteenth century, such as Martin Luther, said we are justified by faith alone but not by a faith that is alone.

This view is at odds with the Roman Catholic schema, which holds that a person must have faith to be justified, but he also needs to have works. So the Catholic view is that faith plus works equals justification. But in the Protestant view, faith equals justification plus works.

ROMAN CATHOLIC VIEW: Faith + Works = Justification

PROTESTANT VIEW: Faith = Justification + Works

In the Protestant view, works are a consequence, a manifestation of the state of grace we are in; thus, they add nothing to justification. The only works of righteousness that serve to justify a sinner are the works of Christ. So when we say that we are justified by faith alone, we mean that we are justified by Christ alone, by His works; our works do not count toward our justification.

Some will say: "I guess that means that I don't have to bear any fruit. I don't have to bring forth any manifestation of righteousness because I'm saved by faith." But remember that the faith that justifies, as James tells us in his epistle (James 2:26) and as Luther argued, is not a dead faith; it is a *fides viva,* a living faith, a vital faith. True faith that connects us to Christ always manifests itself in works, and if there are no works on the right side of the equation, that tells us there is no faith on the left side of the equation. Sadly, if there is no faith on the left side of the equation, then there is no justification on the right side of the equation.

So faith links us to Christ, and if our faith is authentic, we won't come to the last day saying, "Lord, Lord," only to hear Him call us people of lawlessness. No, we will have fruit that demonstrates that our faith is real.

The amount of fruit Christians produce varies. Jesus says the good seed may yield "in one case a hundredfold, in another sixty, and in another thirty" (13:23b). Some true Christians are not as fruitful as other Christians, but every true believer bears some fruit. If he does not, he's not a believer. That's why Jesus says, "You will recognize them by their fruits" (Matt. 7:16a)—not by their professions.

When one is immersed in a Christian subculture that puts a great deal of stress on making decisions, responding to altar calls, and praying the sinner's prayer, it is easy to miss this important point—making a decision to follow Jesus has never converted anyone. This is because it is not a decision that converts a person; it is the power of the Holy Spirit that does so. We get into the kingdom not because we make a decision, walk down an aisle, raise a hand, or sign a card. We get into the kingdom because there is true faith in our hearts.

Don't misunderstand—there's absolutely nothing improper about public professions of faith; they should be made. Everyone who is justified is called to profess that faith; everyone who is a Christian is called to confess Christ before others. The problem comes when we make a public profession of faith the litmus test of our conversion. After all, Jesus speaks of people who honor Him with their lips while their hearts are far from Him (Matt. 15:8). No one has ever been justified by a profession of faith.

Does this mean, then, that the easiest way to solve the problem of assurance of salvation is to examine the fruit of our lives to determine whether it reflects consistency with a profession of faith? There is a definite place for self-examination in the Christian life, and I will say more about that in chapter 4. Yet none of us lives up to the full measure of what we say we believe. If we focus attention simply on our performance, authentic assurance becomes very slippery.

So it is possible to have false assurance, but true assurance can be difficult to acquire. How, then, can we know with certainty that our professions of faith are motivated by the possession of true saving grace? This question is extremely important, for it touches where we live as Christians and has a tremendous impact on our feelings, our comfort, and our behavior as Christians. It is imperative that we settle the matter of whether we are in a state of grace, and the remainder of this booklet will look at how we do that.

Chapter Two

FOUR KINDS
OF PEOPLE

I shared the gospel with a man in Cincinnati and I began
by asking him the first of the two Evangelism Explosion diagnostic questions: "Have you come to the place in
your spiritual life where you know for sure that if you were
to die tonight you would go to heaven?" This man didn't
flinch. He looked me straight in the eye and said: "Oh, no,
I'm sure I'm not saved. I'm sure I'm going to hell." I was
stunned by that response because I had never met a person
who was so certain that hell was his destiny. This man was

living a godless life, he knew he was living a godless life, and he knew the consequences of living an ungodly life, but he didn't care.

When it comes to assurance of salvation, there are four kinds of people in the world. Every living person, without exception, can be assigned to one of these categories. The categories are: 1) those who are saved and know it, 2) those who are saved but do not know it, 3) those (like the man I mentioned above) who are unsaved and know it, and 4) those who are unsaved but do not know it. Let us look more closely at these categories:

People Who Are Saved and Know It

The first category is people who are saved and know it. These people have full assurance that they are in a state of grace. It is a settled matter for them.

You probably have been in discussions where you asked someone a question, he gave some affirmation or assertion, and you replied, "Are you sure?" He said, "Yes, I'm sure." Your next question was, "Are you sure you're sure?" When we talk about certitude or certainty, we're talking not simply about philosophical categories. Instead, we are describing, in a sense, our emotional state with respect to various questions or assertions.

Assurance of truth claims operates on a broad continuum. For example, someone could say to you, "Do you believe that God exists?" There is a range of answers you could give to that question. You could say, "No, I don't," "I don't think so," "I don't know, but I hope so," "Maybe," "Yes, I believe in God," or "Of course I believe in God." Each of those answers describes a different level of intensity of confidence that attends a proposition or an assertion.

So when we speak of assurance of salvation, we're not talking about mathematical certitude, such as belief in the idea that two plus two equals four. We're talking about assurance of a personal state, and the intensity of that assurance vacillates from day to day. There are days when someone might say to me, "R. C., are you sure you're saved?" and I would say, "Absolutely." The next day, if I'm under the burden of guilt, I might say, "You know, I think so." There are ups and downs in the Christian life.

Yet, true assurance survives the doubts, for as we will see, it is based on more than feelings. The person in this category has a foundation from which he can say, "I know whom I have believed and am persuaded that He is able to keep what I have committed to Him until that Day" (2 Tim. 1:12, NKJV).

People Who Are Saved But Do Not Know It

The second category is composed of those who are saved but do not know it. It is possible for a person to be in a state of grace and yet not possess full assurance that he is in such a state. I have already mentioned that some (such as Roman Catholics) challenge the validity of the first group (those who are saved and know it) by claiming that assurance of salvation is generally unattainable. Likewise, others claim that it is impossible to really be in a state of grace and not know it. They argue that the very content of saving faith is a trust in a Savior whom you believe will save you. So if a person thinks he has faith but lacks confidence that Jesus Christ is saving him, does he really have faith at all?

Part of the problem has to do with a popular view of Christianity that insists on a dramatic conversion. Some people do come to Christ that way. Billy Graham, for example, can tell the day and the hour when he became a Christian. He points back to a particular day when he went to an evangelistic meeting after playing in a baseball game. An itinerate evangelist named Mordecai Ham was preaching, and Graham went forward and had a sudden conversion that turned his life upside down. I experienced the same kind of conversion. I know exactly the time when I met Christ. I can tell you the date, the hour, the place, and how it happened. Other people, however, cannot identify even the year when they became Christians. For example, Ruth Graham, Billy's wife, did not know when she was converted.

In the church, we have a tendency to make our own experiences normative for everyone. People who have had sudden, dramatic, Damascus road-type conversions that can be pinpointed to the day and hour sometimes become suspicious of people who have not had that kind of experience. They wonder whether a person who cannot point to a specific day and hour can really be a Christian. At the same time, those who do not know the day and the hour sometimes are suspicious of those who claim that they know exactly when they first believed. The bottom line is this: Nowhere does Scripture say we have to know the exact time of our conversion.

Here's where the plot thickens and becomes a bit problematic. No one is half-regenerate or semi-regenerate; you are either born of the Spirit of God or you are not.

Regeneration, which is that work of God by which we are transferred from the kingdom of darkness into the kingdom of light, is a real work of conversion, and it happens instantly by the work of the Holy Spirit, so that a person is either in that state or not. There is no process of regeneration; it is instantaneous.

But if that's the case, doesn't that raise suspicions about people who cannot state the day and the hour of their conversion? No. We need to distinguish between a *conversion* and a *conversion experience.* Furthermore, we need to recognize that not everyone is instantly aware of the moment when the Spirit of God does His supernatural work within his or her soul. That's why it's very dangerous to create categories by which we evaluate people whose experiences do not match our own.

In fact, as much as I talk about my conversion experience—which, as I said, I can pinpoint to the day and hour—I realize that such an experience may not actually correspond to the work of God in a person's soul. God the Holy Spirit may regenerate a person a week, a month, or even five years before he experiences the reality of what has already happened internally. So even my confidence with regard to a particular date and time of conversion applies only to my experience of conversion, not to the fact of it, because we can fool ourselves in terms of our experience.

Actually, one of the most dangerous things we can do as Christians is to determine our theology by our experience, because no one's experience is normative for the Christian life. We have to determine our theology from the Word of God, not from what we feel. Not only that, we are open to misunderstanding and misinterpreting the meaning and significance of the experiences we go through. That's why we are called to check our experiences against Scripture, so that we define our faith by what Scripture says, not by what we feel or what we experience. If we rest our assurance on an experience and not on the Word of God, we're inviting all kinds of doubts to assail us in our pilgrimages. We need to seek authentic knowledge of our salvation, not just some warm and fuzzy experience.

It is this category of people that is in view when Peter urges believers to diligence in making their calling and election sure (2 Peter 1:3–11). It would be foolish to give such an admonition to people who are already sure. Peter's teaching, then, signifies that people can be in a state of salvation without actually having the assurance of it.

People Who Are Unsaved and Know It

The man I encountered in Cincinnati exemplified this category of people—those who are unsaved and know it. It may seem strange to us that there could be such people, especially since many today assume that everyone goes to heaven when they die. However, the apostle Paul speaks of this category of people at the end of Romans 1. After giving a list of all the various sins and vices that fallen humanity practices, he comes to the conclusion that fallen people not only do these things but encourage others to do them—despite knowing that those who do such things are deserving of death (v. 32).

Paul is telling us in Romans 1 that people do not have to be exposed to biblical preaching to be aware of their lost condition. Through God's natural revelation, as God writes His law on the hearts of people and implants His Word in the human mind by way of conscience, people know that they are culpable for their behavior and that they are out of fellowship with their Creator.

On the surface, many people deny that they are in danger of the wrath of God; they may even deny the existence of God. But the Bible says, "The wicked flee when no one pursues" (Prov. 28:1), so beneath the surface and behind the facade of natural fallen humanity, there is an awareness of serious trouble before God. That's why we have the phenomenon of "foxhole conversions," when people, in the last days of their lives, suddenly sober up, call for the priest or the minister, and attempt to get their eternal life insurance.

You might have heard the story of W. C. Fields, who, when he was lying on his deathbed, astonished those who knew him by leafing through a Bible. One friend said to him, "W. C., what are you doing?" Fields replied, "Looking for loopholes." Though his answer was couched in his typical humor, it is clear that Fields was aware that he was in a very precarious state as he was about to face his Maker.

As difficult as it may be to believe, there are people who are unsaved and know it. They know that they are not in a state of grace, that they are out of fellowship with God, and that they are estranged from Him. We might say they have a negative form of assurance.

People Who Are Unsaved But Do Not Know It

Here's what we have so far: There are those who are saved and know it; there are those who are saved but do not know it; and there are those who are unsaved and know it. These categories are fairly easy to understand.

It's the fourth category that throws a monkey wrench into the whole business of assurance of salvation: those who are unsaved but "know" they are saved. This category consists of people who are not in a state of grace but *think* they are. In short, they have false assurance.

Ligonier Ministries once conducted a tour of Reformation sites, following the footsteps of Martin Luther. We went through the various places in what had been Eastern Europe and East Germany, where Luther carried out his ministry. We went to Erfurt, Wittenberg, Worms, Nuremberg, and other such places. One day we visited a site, and then we were free for lunch on our own. Groups of people from the tour went different directions into the town, and we had instructions as to the place and time we were to regroup for the tour. Well, a group of us wandered around the town and had our lunch, but when we came out of the restaurant, we couldn't remember which way we had come. We said to each other, "How do we get back to the bus?" At that point, one woman in our group said, "I know the way." So she went to the front of the line and started walking through this town, and we all followed her. Soon it was apparent we weren't going in the right direction, and I began to get a little worried. So I said, "Excuse me, Mary, are you sure we're going the right way?" She said, "Yes, I'm positive." I felt relieved, but after a couple more steps she turned around to say, "Of course, I'm always sure, but I'm rarely right."

People who exude confidence that they're on their way to heaven are a bit like that woman. They "know" they are Christians. They're sure of their salvation; it's not something they worry about it. The only problem is that their assurance is false assurance.

That's what creates the tension and the anxiety that we're trying to deal with in this booklet, particularly as we compare groups one and four. Group one, you'll recall, comprises people who are saved and have the assurance of salvation, and group four comprises people who are not saved but nevertheless have an assurance of salvation. As we consider how we can have real assurance, we need to think more on the root causes of false assurance.

Chapter Three

FALSE
ASSURANCE

Our quest for full assurance of salvation is complicated by the fact that there are two very different categories of people who are sure that they're in a state of salvation. The only problem is that one of them is mistaken. These are the people Jesus spoke of in the Sermon on the Mount when He said that some will come to Him at the last day saying, "Lord, Lord." They will come to Jesus fully assured that they belong to Him, but He will turn them away, exposing their assurance as counterfeit.

How can false assurance be possible? How do people arrive at a false sense of assurance? In this chapter, I want to try to answer these questions. There are several different problems, but they basically reduce to two. The first problem, which will be our focus in this chapter, is a faulty understanding of the requirements for salvation. People can misunderstand what salvation entails. We'll look at three of the main errors: universalism, legalism, and various forms of sacerdotalism. The second problem arises when a person has a correct understanding of what salvation entails, but is mistaken as to whether he or she has met the requirements. The final two chapters will help us see how we can accurately evaluate whether we have met the requirements for salvation.

Universalism

The first major error that leads to a false sense of assurance of salvation is universalism. Universalism teaches that everyone is saved and goes to heaven. If a person is convinced of this doctrine of salvation, a simple syllogism will take him from the doctrine of universal salvation to assurance as to his destiny:

Premise 1: Every person goes to heaven.
Premise 2: I am a person.
Conclusion: Therefore, I will go to heaven.

The greatest controversy in the history of the church took place in the sixteenth century between the Roman Catholic Church and the Protestant Reformers over the question of how justification takes place. The issue was whether justification is by faith alone or by some other means. But today, justification by faith alone is not the prevailing view in our culture. Rather, it is the doctrine of justification by death, and universalism carries this idea with it.

I made a brief reference earlier to the first Evangelism Explosion diagnostic question: "Have you come to the place in your spiritual life where you know for sure that if you were to die tonight you would go to heaven?" The second diagnostic question is this: "If you were to die tonight and stand before God, and God were to say to you, 'Why should I let you into My heaven?' what would you say?"

Once, when my son was young, I asked him these two questions. I was delighted that he immediately answered the first question by saying "Yes." But when I asked him the second question, he looked at me as if I had just posed the silliest question he had ever heard. He said, "Well, I would say, 'Because I'm dead.'" What could be simpler? My son was being reared in a home committed to biblical theology, but not only had I failed to communicate justification by faith alone to him, he already had been captured by the pervasive view in our culture that everyone goes to heaven and that all you have to do to get there is to die.

We have so eliminated the last judgment from our theology and expunged any notion of divine punishment or of hell from our thinking (and from the church's thinking) that it is now widely assumed that all a person must do to get to heaven is to die. In fact, the most powerful means of grace for sanctification in our culture is to die, because a sin-blistered sinner is automatically transformed between the morgue and the cemetery, so that when the funeral service is held, the person is presented as a paragon of virtue. His sins seem to have been removed by his death. This is very dangerous business, because the Scriptures warn us that it is appointed for every person once to die, then to face judgment (Heb. 9:27).

People like to think that the threat of a last judgment was invented by fire-and-brimstone evangelists such as Billy Sunday, Dwight L. Moody, Billy Graham, Jonathan

Edwards, and George Whitefield. But no one taught more clearly about the last judgment and a division between heaven and hell than Jesus Himself. In fact, Jesus talked more about hell than He did about heaven, and He warned His hearers that on that last day, every idle word would come into judgment. But if there's anything unredeemed human beings want to repress psychologically, it's that threat of final, comprehensive judgment, because none of them wants to be held accountable for his sins. Therefore, nothing is more appealing to human beings than universalism—the idea that all are saved.

Legalism

The second major error that leads to false assurance is legalism, which is another way of referring to "works righteousness." Legalism teaches that in order to get to heaven, you must obey the law of God and live a good life. In other words, your good deeds will get you into heaven. Many people, mistakenly understanding what God requires, believe they have met the standards God has set for entrance into heaven.

I once served as a trainer for Evangelism Explosion, taking trainees out into the community once or twice a week, talking to people, and asking the diagnostic questions. Afterward, we correlated the answers we received. Ninety percent of the answers fell into the category of works righteousness. When we asked people what they would say if God were to ask them why He should let them enter heaven, most people replied, "I've lived a good life," "I gave a tithe to the church," "I worked with the Boy Scouts," or something along those lines. Their confidence rested on some kind of performance record that they had achieved. Unfortunately, a person's works are a counterfeit basis for assurance. The Scriptures make very clear that no one is justified by the works of the law (Rom. 3:20; Gal. 3:11).

The person who perhaps most embodied this false understanding of salvation was the rich young ruler who encountered Jesus during His earthly ministry (Luke 18:18–30). You may recall that when the rich man came to Jesus, he had compliments dripping from his lips. He said: "Good Teacher, what must I do to inherit eternal life?" He was asking Jesus what was required for salvation.

Before Jesus answered his question about the requirements for salvation, He dealt with the compliment. Jesus asked: "Why do you call me good? No one is good except God alone" (v. 19). Some critics hold that, by virtue of this response, Jesus was denying His goodness and deity. No, Jesus knew very well that this man did not have a clue about the person to whom he was speaking. This man didn't know who Jesus was. He didn't know he was asking a question of God incarnate. All the rich young ruler knew was that he was talking to an itinerate rabbi, and he wanted an answer to a theological question. But Jesus' identity was central to the answer. So Jesus said: "Why do you call Me good? Haven't you read Psalm 14:3: 'They have all turned aside; together they have become corrupt; there is none who does good, not even one'? No one is good except God Himself."

Does that seem absurd? After all, we see people who aren't believers doing good all the time. It all depends on what we mean by "good." The biblical standard of goodness is the righteousness of God, and we are judged both by our behavioral conformity to the law of God and by our internal motivation or desire to obey the law of God.

I see people all around me who aren't believers but who practice what John Calvin called "civic virtue"; that is, they do good things in society. They donate their money for good causes, they help the poor, and they sometimes even sacrifice themselves for others. They do all kinds of wonderful things on the horizontal level (i.e., toward other people), but they do none of it because their hearts have a pure and full love for God. There may be what Jonathan Edwards called an "enlightened self-interest" involved, but it is still self-interest.

I once heard the story of a tragic fire. A building caught on fire, and there was a rush to rescue the people who were in the inferno. The firefighters went in and brought out as many people as they could, but it soon became too dangerous to go back into the building. Then they realized there was a child trapped in the building, and out of the crowd of bystanders, one man, ignoring the danger, rushed into the building as everyone on the street cheered for him. A few moments later, he came back out alive and safe with a bundle in his arms. The people continued to cheer, thinking he had rescued the child. But then they realized he had brought out his life savings and left the child to die.

I do believe it's possible for an unbeliever to rush into a building to save a child, perhaps even at the cost of his life. That's civic virtue motivated by the natural concern we have for one another. But such external virtue isn't enough. When God looks at a human action, He asks, "Does this work proceed from a heart that loves Me fully?" Remember Jesus' commands: "You shall love the Lord your God with all your heart and with all your soul and with all your strength and with all your mind, and your neighbor as yourself" (Luke 10:27). Therefore, if someone obeys the law outwardly, while his or her heart is not fully given to God, then that person's virtue has been tainted. That's why Augustine said even our best virtues are but splendid vices. As long as we're in this body of flesh, sin will taint everything we do. That is what the rich young ruler did not understand. He thought he had achieved the standard.

Paul warns in the New Testament that those who judge themselves by themselves are not wise (1 Cor. 10:12). We can look at one another's performances and think that if we keep ourselves from adultery, murder, embezzlement, or some such egregious sin, then we're doing well. Since we always can find people who are more sinful than we are, it would be easy to conclude that we're doing pretty well.

Such was the mind-set of the rich young ruler who came to Jesus. He thought Jesus was a good man. But Jesus stopped him in his tracks and reminded him of the law: "You know the commandments: 'Do not commit adultery, Do not murder, Do not steal, Do not bear false witness, Honor your father and mother'" (v. 20). That prompted the man to reveal his superficial understanding of the law. He said, "All these I have kept from my youth" (v. 21). In other words, he was saying he had kept the Ten Commandments all his life.

Jesus could have said: "Well, I see you weren't at the Sermon on the Mount when I explained the deeper implications of these laws. You missed that lecture." Or He simply could have told the man, "You haven't kept any of these commands since you got out of your bed this morning." Instead, He used a beautiful pedagogical method to teach this man his error. He said: "One thing you still lack. Sell all that you have and distribute to the poor, and you will have treasure in heaven; and come, follow me" (v. 22).

At this point, Jesus was not teaching a new way of salvation. He was not saying we can be saved by donating our goods to the poor. Neither was He implementing a universal mandate for people to divest themselves of all their private property. He was dealing with this particular man, a rich man whose heart had been completely captured by his wealth. His money was his god, his idol. In essence, Jesus said to him: "You say you have kept all the Ten Commandments. All right, let's check number one: 'You shall have no other gods before me' [Ex. 20:3]. Go, sell everything you have." After that, the man who had been so enthusiastic only moments before began to shake his head. He walked away sorrowful, because he had great possessions (v. 23).

That whole encounter was about goodness. Do we have enough goodness—enough righteousness—to satisfy the demands of a holy God? Every page of the New Testament speaks to the truth that all our righteousness is as filthy rags (Isa. 64:6). The person who is trusting in his righteousness to be saved has a false assurance. We cannot do enough to be saved. We are unprofitable servants (Luke 17:10).

Sacerdotalism

The third common error that produces false assurance is sacerdotalism. This is the view that salvation is accomplished through the priesthood, through the sacraments, and/or through the church. People point to baptism, to the Lord's Supper, or to other rites and say: "I've had these sacraments, which are means of grace. I draw my assurance from having experienced the sacraments."

This is the error the Pharisees committed in biblical days. They assumed that because they were circumcised, they therefore were guaranteed a place in the kingdom of God.

The sacraments are very important. They communicate

the promises of God to us for our salvation. Plus, they are means of grace that help us in our Christian lives. But the sacraments have never saved anyone, and anyone who puts his trust in the sacraments has a false assurance of salvation, because he is trusting in something that neither saves nor can save.

Closely related to this is the idea, which is held by many people, that all a person must do to be saved is to join a church. They assume that since joining a church includes them in the visible body of Christ, they must be part of the invisible church as well. So they put their confidence in their church membership. But membership in a church does not justify anyone; this is another illegitimate and false method of assurance.

Finally, in the so-called evangelical world, we have a few other sources of false assurance: praying the sinner's prayer, raising one's hand at an evangelistic event, going forward during an altar call, or making a decision for Jesus. These are all techniques or methods that are used to call people to repentance and faith. The danger is that people who say the prayer, raise a hand, walk the aisle, or make a decision sometimes end up trusting in that particular act. Outward professions can be deceiving. One can go through the external motions of a *profession* but not truly be in *possession* of the inward reality of salvation.

As you can see, there are many ways in which false assurance can come about. In the next chapter, we will discuss how these counterfeit forms of assurance can be avoided and overcome, and we will begin to explore legitimate methods of attaining assurance that is biblical and real.

Chapter Four

GAINING TRUE
ASSURANCE

When I was in seminary, one of my fellow students polled the students and the faculty members as to whether they were sure of their salvation. More than ninety percent of the respondents said they were not sure. Moreover, they thought it would be arrogant for someone to claim to be sure of his or her salvation. They saw the idea of assurance not as a virtue but as a vice. There was a negative connotation to the very pursuit of assurance of salvation, because it was assumed it would lead to a state of arrogance.

Of course, there's no worse arrogance than to have the assurance of something that we do not, in fact, possess. To be certain of salvation when we are not in a state of salvation is arrogant. Likewise, we are arrogant if we say that assurance is not possible, because then we are slandering the truthfulness of God Himself. If assurance is possible, we are arrogant if we do not seek it.

In considering the sources of false assurance, we saw that one of the most critical problems is an inaccurate understanding of the requirements of salvation. In other words, bad theology can produce false assurance. By the same token, good theology leads to true assurance. Therefore, as we begin to explore how we can gain a true and sound basis for our assurance of salvation, the first place we have to look is theology.

The Command to Seek Assurance

One of the key texts of Scripture in regard to the pursuit of assurance is 2 Peter 1:10–11, where we read: "Therefore, brothers, be all the more diligent to make your calling and election sure, for if you practice these qualities you will never fall. For in this way there will be richly provided for you an entrance into the eternal kingdom of our Lord and Savior Jesus Christ." Here, without ambiguity, the apostolic mandate is for us to inquire into the certainty of our election, and not in a cavalier, casual way. Rather, we are to make our calling and our election sure through a diligent pursuit. The apostle tells us this is very important, then goes on to give us practical reasons to be diligent in making our calling and election sure.

Peter is very concerned about this concept of election. His first epistle is addressed to "those who are elect exiles" (1 Peter 1:1). He writes to the elect and teaches the elect what it means to be elect. Peter explains what election is supposed to look like in our spiritual journey. That's why, in the second epistle, when he addresses the same people, he reminds them how important it is to make their election sure.

Peter's mention of "election" is very important, for it is here that we step through the doorway of theology. Many people do not believe in election, forgetting that it is a biblical concept. Others ask, "How do you know whether you're elect or not?" I tell people who are struggling with the concept of election that I cannot think of a more important question to get resolved in the Christian life than the question of whether we are numbered among the elect. If we have a sound understanding of election, and if we know that we are numbered among the elect, that knowledge provides unbelievable comfort to us as we work out our salvation with fear and trembling (Phil. 2:12) and as we encounter the various afflictions that are placed before us in our Christian lives (2 Tim. 3:12).

In 2 Timothy 1:12, Paul writes, "I know whom I have believed, and I am convinced that he is able to guard until that Day what has been entrusted to me." Paul is talking here about his confidence for his own future because of his knowledge of where he has put his faith. He says he trusts not in his own power to persevere to the end of the race. Instead, his confidence is based on the One in whom he has believed, knowing that One is able to keep him. That is the kind of certainty of election that Peter is telling us to pursue with diligence.

If we are called to make our election sure, then it follows that we are *able* to make our election sure. It is possible for us to know whether we are numbered among the elect. Therefore, we should not postpone seeking assurance till the ends of our lives. We should seek it diligently now. We should get it settled that we are numbered among the elect, that we are in the kingdom of God, that we have been adopted into the Father's house, and that we are truly in Christ, and He in us. But how do we do it? Gaining an accurate understanding of the doctrine of election is a crucial first step.

The Prescient View of Election

As I noted earlier, many people today are hostile to the idea of divine election, and that hostility has led to a number of views on what election involves. For example, some people think that our salvation is the ground of our election. In this perspective, salvation (in a sense) precedes election. We call this the prescient or foreknowledge view of election.

Those who hold this view on election believe that God elects to salvation those who will exercise saving faith. By virtue of His foreknowledge, God looks down the corridor of time and sees who will respond positively to the offer of the gospel and who will not. On the basis of this prior knowledge of what people will do in response to the gospel message, He makes His decree of election. When He sees people exercising faith and entering into a state of salvation, He elects them on that basis.

I do not believe this view of election is biblical or that

it explains election. In fact, I think it fundamentally denies the biblical teaching on election. I say this because the foreknowledge perspective on election makes the deciding factor in salvation, in the final analysis, something that we do rather than the grace and mercy of God. I think people who take this foreknowledge view of election invariably struggle with their assurance, because their assurance is ultimately tied to their performance.

As I understand the Scriptures, election is unto salvation. In this view, if you are elect, you will be saved, and if you are saved, that is the clearest sign that you are numbered among the elect. Let me say it another way: None who are saved are not elect, and none who are elect fail to be saved. Salvation flows out of election, so if we want to be sure of our salvation, we need to know whether we are numbered among the elect.

In Peter's teaching, we see why it is so important that we be diligent in making our calling and election sure. If we are sure that we are numbered among the elect, we can be certain with respect to our salvation, not only for today but for the future as well. This is true because election does not simply make salvation possible, it guarantees the salvation of the elect. In other words, the purpose of God in election is to save the elect. That purpose cannot and will not be frustrated.

There is a Scripture passage in which I take great comfort, even though it is not usually mentioned in this context. It is found in the Gospel of John, in the middle of Jesus' High Priestly Prayer for His disciples and for those who would believe in Him in future generations. In fact, this has been a passage of great encouragement for the church throughout the ages. Jesus says:

> "I have manifested Your name to the men whom You have given Me out of the world. They were Yours, You gave them to Me, and they have kept Your word. Now they have known that all things which You have given Me are from You. For I have given to them the words which You have given Me; and they have received them, and have known surely that I came forth from You; and they have believed that You sent Me.
>
> "I pray for them. I do not pray for the world but for those whom You have given Me, for they are Yours. And all Mine are Yours, and Yours are Mine, and I am glorified in them. Now I am no longer in

the world, but these are in the world, and I come to You. Holy Father, keep through Your name those whom You have given Me, that they may be one as We are. While I was with them in the world, I kept them in Your name. Those whom You gave Me I have kept; and none of them is lost except the son of perdition, that the Scripture might be fulfilled." (John 17:6–12, NKJV)

In this prayer, Jesus says that the Father has given a certain group of people to Him. These people are redeemed by the Son, because all whom the Father gives to the Son come to the Son and are kept by Him (John 6:37, 39–40, 44). When Jesus speaks of people who are given to Him by the Father, He is referring to the elect. The elect whom the Father gives to the Son are preserved by the Son. That is the basis of our true assurance, not our own ability to persevere.

We talk about the perseverance of the saints, and I believe that the saints do in fact persevere, but they persevere because they are preserved by God. So it's better to speak of the preservation of the saints than the perseverance of the saints. We hear this in Jesus' appeal to the Father to keep those who have been given to Him.

The *Ordo Salutis*

When we look further at the relationship between election and salvation, we need to be concerned with what theologians call the *ordo salutis*, or "the order of salvation." The *ordo salutis* has to do with the order in which various events occur that lead to our redemption, specifically the logical order rather than the temporal order.

Here's what I mean by that distinction. We believe that we are justified by faith alone. But how long after we possess true saving faith are we justified? Is it five seconds, five minutes, five months, five years? No, we say that justification and faith are coterminous with respect to time. The very moment we have true faith, in that same instant, God receives us as justified people. But we still say that faith comes before justification, even though they occur at the same time. Faith precedes justification logically. In other words, since our justification depends on and rests on faith, faith is the prerequisite, the necessary condition that has to be present for justification to take place. So faith is logically necessary for justification. It precedes justification, not in time, but in terms of logical necessity. So when we talk about the order of salvation, keep in mind that what we have in view are the distinctions with respect to prerequisites on the basis of logical necessity.

In Romans 8, we have one of the most famous and beloved verses in all of the New Testament: "And we know that for those who love God all things work together for good, for those who are called according to his purpose" (v. 28). Notice that this promise that all things work together for good is for those who love God, those who are described as the ones who are called according to His purpose.

That's a special kind of calling. The Bible speaks about the call of the gospel that goes out to everyone—what we call the outward call or the external call. Not everyone who hears this call is saved. We also speak of the inward call, the call of God in the person, in the heart, which is a work of God the Holy Spirit, and which call is effectual. In this call, the Holy Spirit opens the hearts of believers, working within to bring about the purpose of God. It is this call Paul has in view in Romans 8:28. All of the elect receive this inward call, as becomes very clear in the following verses.

Let's look at the first half of verse 29: "For those whom he foreknew he also predestined to be conformed to the image of his Son." Paul is talking here about the purposes of God with respect to salvation, and he begins by mentioning

God's foreknowledge. He tells us that those whom God foreknew, He predestined. What was the goal of this predestination? It was that those God foreknew would be conformed to the image of Christ.

In verse 30, we encounter what we call "the golden chain": "And those whom he predestined he also called, and those whom he called he also justified, and those whom he justified he also glorified." This is an abbreviated version of the order of salvation. There are other aspects to salvation besides those mentioned here; Romans 8:30 hits the highlights, as it were. For instance, sanctification is not in this list. Rather, this list includes (going back to verse 29) first, foreknowledge; second, predestination; third, calling; fourth, justification; and fifth, glorification.

It is very important for our understanding of assurance to grasp what is going on in this order of salvation. As I noted, Paul is referring to a logical order, and it starts with foreknowledge. The prescient view of election that I mentioned earlier is popular because people come to this text and say: "Aha! The first step is foreknowledge. That means election or predestination is based on something that God knows about people in advance." But the text does not say that. In fact, as Paul elaborates on this in

Romans 9, he precludes that possibility. According to the Reformed understanding of election, the people who are elect according to God's decrees are not nameless ciphers. For God to elect someone, He must have some idea of whom He is electing. So foreknowledge must precede predestination, because God is predestining specific individuals whom He loves and chooses.

The next logical event is predestination. Paul tells us that those whom God foreknew He also predestined. It is unstated but clearly understood here that all who are in the category of the foreknown are predestined. Of course, God's foreknowledge, in general, includes all people, not just the elect. But Paul is speaking here about God's foreknowledge of His elect. How do we know that? Because Paul declares that all whom God foreknows, in the sense that He foreknows them here, are predestined, and all who are predestined are called, and all who are called are justified. That is the crucial point. If all who are called are justified, Paul cannot possibly be referring to the external call. He must be speaking of the internal call, because all who receive this particular call receive justification, just as all who are justified are glorified.

So if I want to know whether I am going to be glorified—that is, whether I'm going to be saved in the final analysis—I need to determine whether I'm justified. If I'm justified, I know I'm going to be glorified. In other words, if I'm justified now, I have nothing to worry about—He who has begun a good work in me is going to finish it to the end (Phil. 1:6).

Calling Relates to Assurance

Where does calling fit into our assurance? I'll say more about this in the next chapter, but for now let me say that if the calling Paul mentions in Romans 8:29–30 has reference to the operation of the Holy Ghost on the soul that prepares us for faith and justification, and if we know we have received this call, we know we are elect.

But how do we know whether we are called? Paul provides the answer in Ephesians 2:

And you He made alive, who were dead in trespasses and sins, in which you once walked according to the course of this world, according to the prince of the power of the air, the spirit who now works in the sons of disobedience, among whom also we all once conducted ourselves in the lusts of our flesh, fulfilling the desires of the flesh and of the mind, and were by nature children of wrath, just as the others. But God, who is rich in mercy, because of His great love with which He loved us, even when we were dead in trespasses, made us alive together with Christ (by grace you have been saved), and raised us up together, and made us sit together in the heavenly places in Christ Jesus, that in the ages to come He might show the exceeding riches of His grace in His kindness toward us in Christ Jesus. For by grace you have been saved through faith, and that not of yourselves; it is the gift of God, not of works, lest anyone should boast. For we are His workman-ship, created in Christ Jesus for good works, which God prepared beforehand that we should walk in them. (Eph. 2:1–10, NKJV)

In this brief summary, Paul is focusing on the work of the Holy Spirit by which we are "made alive," a work we under-stand theologically as our rebirth or regeneration. Jesus told Nicodemus that rebirth must occur before anyone can see the kingdom, let alone enter it (John 3:3, 5). And rebirth is tied to this internal calling. So as we seek assurance, we can know we're numbered among the elect, because without election, this work of the Holy Ghost could never take place in our souls.

So all who are elect will become, at some point in this life, regenerate by the Holy Spirit. Likewise, all who are regenerate are numbered among the elect. So if you can be sure of your regeneration, you can be sure of your election; and if you're sure of your election, you can be sure of your salvation.

Therefore, it is critical that we understand what regeneration is. There is massive confusion in the Christian world about the nature of this act of the Spirit. People who call themselves evangelicals in America believe very different things about what happens to a person when the Holy Spirit regenerates him from spiritual death to spiritual life. That's why having a sound doctrine of regeneration is critical to having a full assurance of our state of grace and our relationship to God. So in the last chapter, I want to look at the work of God the Holy Spirit in our lives as the most important foundation for genuine assurance of salvation.

Chapter Five

THE SOURCE
OF FULL ASSURANCE

P olls conducted by organizations such as Gallup and
the Barna Group routinely find that tens of millions of
Americans claim to be "born-again Christians." Unfortunately, many of those people have a woeful understanding
of what it means to be born again. If asked, they will say,
"Well, a born-again Christian is someone who made a
decision of an evangelistic sort" or "A born-again person is
someone who has said the sinner's prayer." Yet these actions

are not true indications that a person has been born again; as we have seen, it is possible to make a profession of faith without being regenerated.

To be born again means to be changed by the supernatural operation of God the Holy Spirit. Understanding this is critical for our assurance of salvation.

In the previous chapter, we looked at Ephesians 2, where we saw a strong contrast between our experience before and after the regeneration of the Holy Spirit. Prior to regeneration, we follow "the course of this world, according to the prince of the power of the air, the spirit who now works in the sons of disobedience . . . fulfilling the desires of the flesh and of the mind" (vv. 2–3a, NKJV). That describes the life of the fallen person who is not reborn. But after the new birth, we are "no longer strangers and foreigners, but fellow citizens with the saints and members of the household of God" (v. 19, NKJV).

What takes place in regeneration? What is the change that is effected by the operation of the Spirit in our souls?

Part of the dispute about regeneration focuses on differences in our understanding of original sin. All professing Christians believe that mankind experienced some kind of a fall and that there's something wrong with our

constituent nature. We all believe that we are corrupt crea-
tures. But there are massive differences with respect to the
degree of that fall—in other words, with respect to the
degree of moral corruption that arose as a result of the fall.

There are Christians who believe that, yes, man is
fallen, but there remains in the soul, as corrupt as the soul
may be, what I call a small "island of righteousness" that
is unaffected by the fall. From this island of righteousness, a person still has the power to cooperate with God's
offer of grace before he or she is regenerated. However,
I cannot find this idea anywhere in Scripture. When we
read Scripture's teaching on our natural state, we see such
descriptions as "bondage to corruption" (Rom. 8:21),
"dead in transgressions and sins" (Eph. 2:1), and "children
of wrath" (Eph. 2:3). Historically, the church has understood these statements to mean that the unregenerate
person has a moral bent, a bias against God. By nature,
the Scriptures tell us, we are at enmity with God, and the
word *enmity* is a description of a hostile attitude. Before
we are regenerated, we are disinclined toward the things
of God. We have no genuine affection for Christ; there is
no love for God in our hearts.

How, then, can we know that we are regenerate?

Do You Love Jesus?

At a practical level, people who are struggling with their assurance of salvation often approach me and ask, "How can I know I am saved?" In response, I ask them three questions.

First I ask, "Do you love Jesus perfectly?" Every person to whom I have asked that question has responded candidly, "No, I don't." That's why they are not sure of the state of their souls; they know there are deficiencies in their affection for Christ, because they know that if they loved Christ perfectly, they would obey Him perfectly. Jesus said, "If you love me, you will keep my commandments" (John 14:15). So as soon as we disobey one of His commandments, that's a signal to us that we do not love Him perfectly.

Second, when a person acknowledges that he doesn't love Jesus perfectly, I ask, "Do you love Him as much as you ought to?" The person usually gives me a strange look and says, "Well, no, of course, I don't." That's right; if the answer to the first question is no, the answer to the second question has to be no, because we're supposed to love Him perfectly, but we don't. Therein lies the tension that we experience about our salvation.

Third, I ask, "Well, do you love Jesus *at all*?" Before the person answers, I usually add that I'm asking about his love for the biblical Christ, the Christ whom we encounter in the pages of Holy Scripture. Why do I say that?

Many years ago, I taught at the Young Life Institute in Colorado Springs, Colorado, and I did a lot of work in those days with and for Young Life. When I was training staff in Colorado, I said: "Let me warn you about one grave danger of this ministry. I don't know personally of any ministry to young people in the world that's more effective than Young Life at getting next to kids, getting involved in their issues, getting involved in their problems, ministering to kids where they are, and knowing how to get them to respond. That's the greatest strength of this organization—and it's also your greatest weakness. Because Young Life, as a ministry, makes Christianity so attractive to kids, it would be easy for kids to be converted to Young Life without ever being converted to Christ."

In just the same way, it's possible to love a caricature of Jesus rather than Jesus Himself. So when I ask people "Do you love Jesus at all?" I'm not asking whether they love a Christ who is a hero for kids or a Christ who is a good moral teacher. I'm asking whether they love the Christ who appears in Scripture.

Now if someone can say "Yes" to that third question, that's where theology comes in. Consider this question: "Is it possible for an unregenerate person to have any true affection for Christ?" My answer is no; affection for Christ is a result of the Spirit's work. That is what regeneration is all about; that is what the Spirit does in quickening. God the Holy Spirit changes the disposition of our souls and the inclination of our hearts. Before regeneration, we are cold, hostile, or indifferent (which is the worst kind of hostility) to the things of God, having no honest affection for Him, because we are in the flesh, and the flesh does not love the things of God. Love for God is kindled by the regenerating power of the Holy Spirit, who pours the love of God into our hearts (Rom. 5:5).

So if a person can answer "Yes" when I ask whether he has an affection for Christ, even though he may not love Jesus as much as he ought to (i.e., perfectly), that assures me the Spirit has done this transforming work in his soul. This is so because we do not have the power in our flesh to conjure up any true affection for Jesus Christ.

A False View of Regeneration

There are views of regeneration out there that won't give you that kind of assurance. One of the most popular views of regeneration in the evangelical world today holds that at regeneration the Holy Spirit simply comes into your life; He indwells you. But even after regeneration (according to this view), you have to respond to the Spirit, to cooperate with Him and put Him in charge of your life, because it's possible for you to be regenerate, indwelt by the Holy Spirit, and yet never bring forth any fruits of obedience. You can become what some call "a carnal Christian."

When the New Testament uses the word *carnal*, it means we start out being purely carnal. When we are in the flesh, the Holy Spirit changes the disposition of our hearts. He doesn't immediately annihilate the flesh; the carnal dimension still wages war with us. The flesh battles with the Spirit throughout the entire Christian life, and there are times when we are more or less carnal (Gal. 5:17). There is no dispute about that. However, some use the term "carnal Christian" to describe a person who remains unchanged by the presence of the Holy Ghost. When the term is used this way, it does not describe a Christian but an unregenerate person.

So I reject this view of regeneration out of hand as involving no regeneration at all, because although the Spirit supposedly enters into the person's life, it does not produce a supernatural work of grace that changes the inclination and disposition of the soul. The person remains the same in his soul as he was before the Spirit came. It is critical to understand that regeneration is something that the Holy Spirit does that really and truly changes a person; it changes the very disposition of his soul. If a person is truly regenerate and manifests faith, it is impossible for that person not to bring forth some measure of obedience.

The "Earnest" of the Spirit

We have seen that regeneration is the work of the Holy Spirit by which the inclination of the soul is changed. But not only does the Holy Spirit change us via regeneration, He does other things that are important to our assurance of salvation. Second Corinthians 5:1–5 reads:

For we know that if the tent that is our earthly home is destroyed, we have a building from God, a house not made with hands, eternal in the heavens. For in this tent we groan, longing to put on our heavenly dwelling, if indeed by putting it on we may not be found naked. For while we are still in this tent, we groan, being burdened—not that we would be unclothed, but that we would be further clothed, so that what is mortal may be swallowed up by life. He who has prepared us for this very thing is God, who has given us the Spirit as a guarantee.

Other translations of the Bible render the word *guarantee* as *earnest*. The language here comes from the commercial world of the ancient Greeks. Today, about the only time we hear the word *earnest* used as a noun is in the arena of real estate. If you are interested in buying a home and you want to sign the initial contract for the sellers to take the home off the market, they will ask you to give what some people call "earnest money." They don't want to deal with people who are just playing around with the idea of buying a house; they want people who are "earnest" about it—in other words, people who are serious about it. The idea in 2 Corinthians 5:5 is that the Spirit, when He regenerates us, not only changes the disposition of our hearts and the inclination of our souls, He becomes for us the earnest, or the guarantee, of full and final payment.

When I buy something over a period of time, I have to make a down payment. Now we know that there are many people who enter into contracts, make a few payments, then renege. Sometimes a person's house is foreclosed or his car is repossessed because he fails to keep the terms of a contract. With the down payment, he promises to pay the whole amount, but people don't always come through. However, when God makes a down payment on something, that down payment is His word. It is His promise that He will, in fact, pay the whole amount. This is the language Paul is using when he says that when we're born of the Spirit, not only does the Spirit change our hearts, our souls, and our wills, but He gives to us the pledge—the guarantee—that the fullness of our salvation will be realized.

People overlook this fact when they say, "Well, I may be saved today, but tomorrow I could lose it." This ignores the biblical truth that God finishes what He starts. When He makes a down payment, the rest will be paid—guaranteed. This is a firm basis for our assurance.

The Seal of God the King

Let's take another example, this time from 2 Corinthians 1:

> Because I was sure of this, I wanted to come to you first, so that you might have a second experience of grace. I wanted to visit you on my way to Macedonia, and to come back to you from Macedonia and have you send me on my way to Judea. Was I vacillating when I wanted to do this? Do I make my plans according to the flesh, ready to say "Yes, yes" and "No, no" at the same time? As surely as God is faithful, our word to you has not been Yes and No. For the Son of God, Jesus Christ, whom we proclaimed among you, Silvanus and Timothy and I, was not Yes and No, but in him it is always Yes. For all the promises of God find their Yes in him. That is why it is through him that we utter our Amen to God for his glory. (vv. 15–20)

What is Paul saying here? Simply that God does not vacillate on His promises. He does not say "Yes" and "No." All of His promises, the apostle tells us, are firmly established by the divine character, which is marked by faithfulness.

Then Paul goes on to say, "And it is God who establishes us with you in Christ, and has anointed us, and who has also put his seal on us and given us his Spirit in our hearts as a guarantee" (2 Cor. 1:21–22). There it is again—the guarantee of the Spirit. But not only do we have the guarantee or the earnest of the Spirit, we also, Paul tells us—and he repeats this idea later in Ephesians— are sealed by the Holy Ghost. The Greek word for "seal" is *sphragis*.

Perhaps you've seen movies of the Middle Ages that show the various customs of monarchs. When a king sent out a decree to be posted in the villages, a wax seal was affixed to the proclamation. That seal was the sign of the king, which was based on his signet ring. Etched inside of his signet ring was a certain shape or form that contained the sign of his signature. So if a document, a proclamation, or an edict contained the seal in wax from the king's signet ring, that was irrefutable testimony of its authenticity. Paul tells us here in 2 Corinthians that the King of the universe places His indelible mark on the soul of every one of His people. He not only gives us an ironclad guarantee, He seals us for the day of redemption.

The Internal Witness of the Holy Spirit

Finally, in Romans 8, we read these encouraging words:

> For as many as are led by the Spirit of God, these are sons of God. For you did not receive the spirit of bondage again to fear, but you received the Spirit of adoption by whom we cry out, "Abba, Father." The Spirit Himself bears witness with our spirit that we are children of God, and if children, then heirs— heirs of God and joint heirs with Christ, if indeed we suffer with Him, that we may also be glorified together. (Rom. 8:14–17, NKJV)

As we study our lives and hearts, the fruit of the Spirit (Gal. 5:22–24), and the measure of change in our lives, we must be honest in our evaluation of what's going on inside of us and through us. But in the final analysis, the bed-rock of our assurance of salvation comes from the internal testimony of the Holy Spirit, for He bears witness to our spirits (inside us) that we are the children of God.

How do we know that this testimony to our spirits is from the Holy Spirit and not from an evil spirit? How does the Holy Spirit confirm in our hearts that we are the children of God? The Spirit bears witness to our spirits through the Word. The farther we get away from the Word, the less assurance we will experience in this life. The more we are in the Word of God, the more the Spirit who inspired the Word and who illumines it for us will use the Word to confirm in our souls that we are truly His, that we are indeed among the children of God.

About the Author

Dr. R.C. Sproul is the founder and chairman of Ligonier Ministries, an international Christian discipleship organization located near Orlando, Fla. He also serves as copastor at Saint Andrew's Chapel in Sanford, Fla., as chancellor of Reformation Bible College, and as executive editor of *Tabletalk* magazine. His teaching can be heard around the world on the daily radio program *Renewing Your Mind*.

During his distinguished academic career, Dr. Sproul helped train men for the ministry as a professor at several theological seminaries.

He is author of more than one hundred books, including *The Holiness of God*, *Chosen by God*, *The Invisible Hand*, *Faith Alone*, *Everyone's a Theologian*, *Truths We Confess*, *The Truth of the Cross*, and *The Prayer of the Lord*. He also served as general editor of the *Reformation Study Bible* and has written several children's books, including *The Knight's Map*. Dr. Sproul and his wife, Vesta, make their home in Sanford.

Further your Bible study with *Tabletalk* magazine, another learning tool from R.C. Sproul.

....

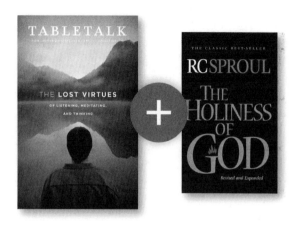

Sign up for a free 3-month trial of *Tabletalk* magazine and we will send you R.C. Sproul's *The Holiness of God*

TryTabletalk.com/CQ